FFESTINIOG
IN COLOUR
1955 to 1982

Hugh Ballantyne

Series editor Vic Mitchell

MP Middleton Press

Front Cover: This young lady has an excellent vantage point in August 1972 on the pavement at Minffordd to watch the unique sight of a working Fairlie double-engine **Merddin Emrys** *leaving the station with a train to Portmadoc. (Robin Patrick)*

Rear Cover (upper): The oldest steam locomotive in regular service in Great Britain is 0-4-0ST **Prince**. *It is seen here at Boston Lodge in October 1980, shortly after it had been re-boilered and converted to oil burning. The engine was built by 0-4-0T by George England & Co at New Cross, London in 1863. (Festiniog Railway Archives)*

Rear Cover (lower): On a bright day in November 1971, **Merddin Emrys** *stands alongside the water tank and coal stack at Portmadoc Harbour station. (Festiniog Railway Archives)*

Published July 2012

ISBN 978 1 908174 25 3

© Middleton Press, 2012

Design Deborah Esher

Published by
      Middleton Press
      Easebourne Lane
      Midhurst
      West Sussex
      GU29 9AZ
Tel: 01730 813169
Fax: 01730 812601
Email: info@middletonpress.co.uk
www.middletonpress.co.uk

Printed in the United Kingdom by Henry Ling Limited, at the Dorset Press, Dorchester, DT1 1HD

INDEX

ACKNOWLEDGEMENTS

In addition to those names appearing in the photographic credits I would particularly like to thank Adrian Gray, the Festiniog Railway Company Hon. Archivist and custodian of the photographic collection for generously allowing me full access to their files of colour images. I am also grateful to John Alexander, Godfrey Croughton, Peter Johnson, Norman Langridge and Geoffrey Monks for their help and guidance and likewise encouragement from my publisher, and as ever, Toni, my very supportive wife. Allan Garraway and Vic Mitchell have both read the draft. They are the surviving founder members of the Festiniog Railway Society. The former was general manager of the FR for the years covered by this album and the latter became a FRS director and later founded Middleton Press.

I. The FR in 1978 with the spiral complete and the new route open to Tanygrisiau.

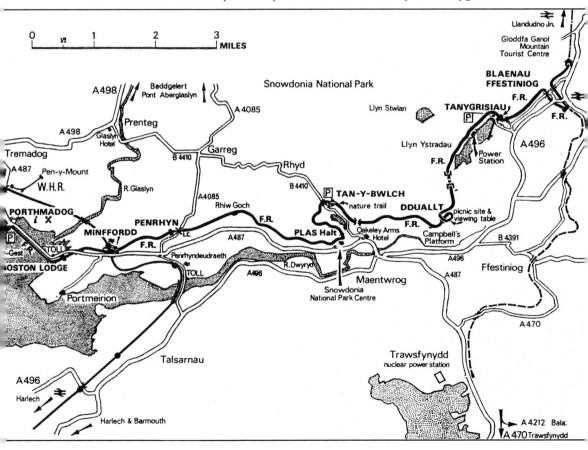

INTRODUCTION

    This album is to commemorate, thirty years since the Festiniog Railway in its preservation guise, achieved its stated ambition of reopening the moribund railway back to Blaenau Ffestiniog in 1982. Today, one cannot visualise how nature and the weather reclaimed a railway which had lain dormant for nine years and the enormity of the task, both in physical and financial terms, required to get it working again. I shall never forget my first sight which prompted me to take the photograph overleaf at Portmadoc Harbour station on a bright October morning in 1951 of the desolate and forlorn stock rotting away and rusty slate wagons hidden in undergrowth, and thinking the railway could never work again. How wrong I was!

    This album sets out the illustrations in mainly geographical order from the coast at Porthmadog up to Blaenau Ffestiniog during the 27 years of restoration. There are few colour pictures of good quality that appear to have been taken in the 1950s, probably because colour photography was still something of a novelty, and film speed of transparency film was slow, making exposures difficult except in the very best sunlight conditions. Most colour pictures were prints, and processing by numerous laboratories was of variable quality, so it has been an extensive exercise scouring images which I hope you, the reader, will find interesting.

    Please note that the English spelling of certain place names, until superseded by the change to Welsh spelling which came about in 1972, has been used where appropriate to the date of the picture.

    Many of the tickets are from the pre-closure period, but some types were also used after the reopening.

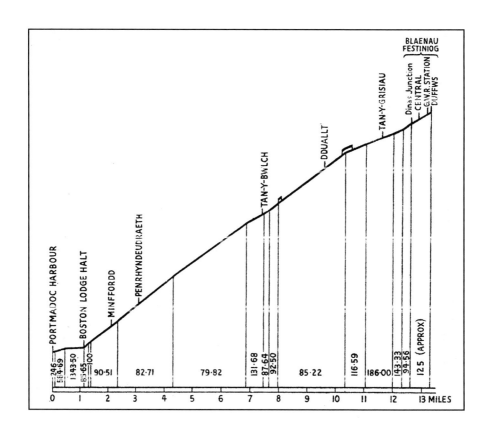

HISTORICAL BACKGROUND

The railway is correctly known as the Festiniog Railway Company as defined by its Act of Parliament which received the Royal Assent on 23rd May 1832. The railway was constructed between 1833 and 1836 to transport slate from the quarries centered around the town of Blaenau Ffestiniog 700 feet above sea level and some fourteen miles from the wharves on the coast at Portmadoc.

The railway was built on a constant falling gradient (except the half mile stretch on either side of the Moelwyn spur until the opening of the tunnel in 1842) so that loaded wagons could run all the way downhill by gravity. The empties were hauled back by horses which had travelled on the downhill trains in special 'dandy' wagons. After the opening of the tunnel trains ran the whole distance down by gravity, until increasing traffic in 1863 required horses to be replaced by steam locomotives to haul the empties back uphill.

Still more powerful locomotives were required and in 1869 Robert Fairlie's patent design double-bogie engine *Little Wonder* entered service. This type of locomotive on such a narrow gauge attracted world-wide interest and its successor double-engines have become the most well known feature of the FR.

Later, as more slate traffic was being transported by the two standard gauge railways now serving Blaenau Ffestiniog, it meant traffic was being siphoned off the FR. With the lessening demand for slate as a roofing material and despite summer tourist traffic, there was a steady decline in receipts.

Following the outbreak of World War II, passenger trains ceased on 15th September 1939 and slate trains followed after the War on 1st August 1946, except for the short section from Duffws to the LMS goods yard at Blaenau Ffestiniog. This provided the railway with minimal receipts and so it was able to retain its manager, Robert Evans, throughout the moribund years.

Harbour station in October 1951 (Author)

From 1948 some interest was shown in trying to revive the railway, but it was not until my friend and fellow young enthusiast, Leonard Heath Humphrys, organised a meeting in Bristol in 1951, the wake-up call which led to the formation of the Festiniog Railway Society. A business man, Mr. Alan Pegler, gained control of the FR in 1954, new directors were appointed and the controlling interest was passed to the Festiniog Railway Trust. Mr. Evans retired in 1955 and Allan Garraway became manager. A very small staff and a slowly increasing number of members set about the daunting task to reopen the railway stage by stage.

Not only were there huge demands on repairing the track, infrastructure and restoring stock, but in 1954 British Electricity Authority's scheme for a pumped water storage installation near Tanygrisiau meant that part of the railway above Moelwyn Tunnel would become submerged by a reservoir. The Railway opposed the Parliamentary Bill, but the Authority regarded the Directors and members as mere amateurs playing at trains and subsequently the section of track it needed was compulsory acquired in 1956.

The railway's avowed intention was to re-open back to Blaenau, and, in 1962, a route around the south east side of the reservoir, by means of a spiral at Ddaullt had been surveyed. Work started in 1965 by volunteers who became known as the 'Deviationists' and, during this time, the battle for compensation was settled in 1971. The FR was awarded £106,000 and an alternative route around the north west side of the reservoir was agreed. The legal case took over 18 years to conclude and is one of the longest in legal history.

However, the settlement required the railway to construct a new shorter Moelwyn Tunnel and bridge the four power station water pipes before regaining the old track at Tanygrisiau in 1978. The final section to Blaenau Ffestiniog also needed much clearance along the hillside and a road bridge had to be reinstated.

Finally, at Blaenau Ffestiniog there was a scheme to benefit the town by building a joint BR/FR station near the town centre which, together with road improvements adopted by the County Council, gave the FR a new and better located station. With financial support the final push became a joint effort by volunteers, engineering contractors and public bodies which culminated in the FR reopening throughout on 25th May 1982. Thus the first pioneering era from 1955 to 1982 had been achieved and this album is to acknowledge that magnificent effort.

Reopening Dates

Boston Lodge	23 July 1955	Ddaullt	6 April 1968
Minffordd	19 May 1956	Llyn Ystradau	25 June 1977
Penrhyn	20 April 1957	Tanygrisiau	24 June 1978
Tan-y-Bwlch	5 April 1958	Blaenau Ffestiniog	25 May 1982

The August 1957 timetable was the first from a revived railway to be in a national publication. This extract is from *Bradshaw's History* (Middleton Press 2012). The Talyllyn Railway had been in Bradshaw's timetables for many decades.

Table 9a   PORTMADOC (Harbour). MINFFORDD and PENRHYNDEUDRAETH—Festiniog

Miles	Up	Week Days only							Down	Week Days only							
		am A	non A	pm	pm	pm	pm	pm B		am A	pm A	pm	pm	pm	pm	pm B	
—	Portmadoc (H'bour) dep	11 0	12 0	2 0	3 0	4 0	5 0	7 30	Penrhyndeudraeth.. arr	1130	1230	2 30	3 30	4.30	5 30	8 0	
2	Minffordd	1112	1212	2 12	3 12	4 12	5 12	7 42	Minffordd	1138	1238	2 38	3 38	4 38	5 38	8 8	
—	Penrhyndeudraeth . arr	1120	1220	2 20	3 20	4 20	5 20	7 50	Portmadoc (H'bour) arr	1150	1250	2 50	3 50	4 50	5 50	8 20	

A Runs 15th July to 7th Sept.
B Tues., Weds., Thurs. and Sats. 16th July to 7th Sept.

All Trains call at Pen Cob, Boston Lodge and Pen-y-Bryn Halts By Request

This table appeared in the February 1961 issue of *Bradshaw's Guide*. This was the last year in which this splendid timetable was published.

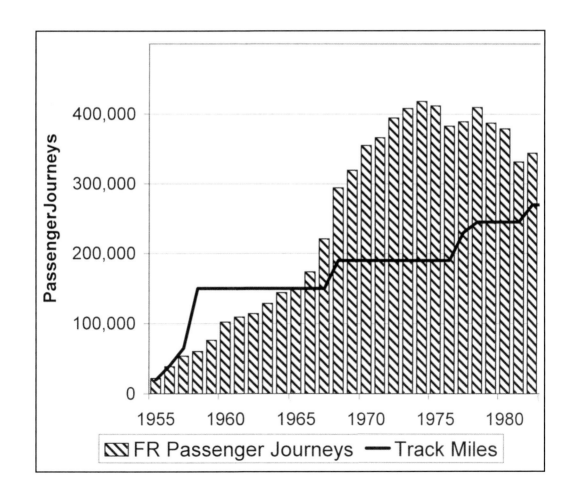

PORTMADOC

1.   After considerable effort for the public opening of the railway on 23rd July 1955, the honour of operating the train service for the first two weeks fell to the 1917 built Simplex, until 0-4-0-ST *Prince* took over the service on 3rd August. Here, the Simplex with coaches nos 12 and 23 in green and ivory livery, is preparing to leave for Boston Lodge during the first week. This had become the first public train service on the Festiniog Railway since 15th September 1939. (J.B.Snell)

2.   Portmadoc seen in 1958, still with grass covered track, but now with two operational steam locomotives. On the right is the 1886 built *Taliesin* and the first of the Fairlie double engines to be put back into traffic in 1957, with *Prince* ready to shunt some of the earliest carriages built by Brown Marshalls of Birmingham in 1863/64. (Festiniog Railway Archives)

3.   On 22nd May 1963, the Railway celebrated the centenary of steam haulage and included in the event at Portmadoc, in front of a large crowd of spectators, was a horse shunting slate wagon. This was to demonstrate that prior to the introduction of steam locomotives, they were the means of moving wagons off the downhill gravity trains and their return uphill to the quarries. (Michael Whitehouse)

4.   *Prince* is shunting at Portmadoc on 7th July 1963, with the former landmark building of the Britannia Foundry seen on the opposite side of the road. *Prince* was one of the first four steam locomotives built by George England of London for the railway in 1863 and originally named *The Prince*. It had major rebuilds in 1892 and 1921 and when reassembled in 1955 it had the benefit of a new boiler, which had been ordered in 1940, but not delivered until 1945. (Alan Wild)

FESTINIOG RAILWAY
PORTMADOC to
TAN-Y-BWLCH
FARE AS ADVERTISED
FIRST CLASS
Issued subject to the Conditions contained in the Company's Notices Exhibited at their Premises.
0559   0559

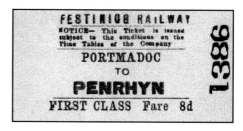

FESTINIOG RAILWAY
NOTICE— This Ticket is issued subject to the conditions on the Time Tables of the Company
PORTMADOC
TO
PENRHYN
FIRST CLASS   Fare 8d
1386

5.　　In the early 1960s, a fund was raised to purchase the first Beyer-Garratt. It was built by Beyer, Peacock of Manchester in 1909, as an 0-4-0+0-4-0 numbered K1, for the North East Dundas Tramway in Tasmania. This line closed in 1929 and the engine was returned to Beyer, Peacock and preserved at their works until purchased by the Festiniog Railway in February 1966. and stored for future use. Shortly after arrival from Manchester, K1 was placed on display opposite the station at Portmadoc where it is seen on 8th May 1966. A train hauled by *Linda* is starting across the Cob towards Boston Lodge. (Festiniog Railway Archives)

6.　　On a summer's afternoon in September 1966, *Blanche* is looking immaculate and gets an admiring glance before departure to Tan-y-Bwlch with carriages in the ivory and green and the new varnished livery. It was later found the latter livery did not weather evenly and was replaced by a cherry colour scheme. (Festiniog Railway Archives)

7.   One of the two Penrhyn Quarry 0-4-0STs acquired by the Festiniog Railway is seen taking water from the 1956 built water tank at Portmadoc. *Blanche* was built by the Hunslet Engine Co in 1893 and was one of three locomotives built to work the Penrhyn Quarry Railway main line. It came to the FR in 1963, a year after its sister engine *Linda*. In 1965 *Blanche* was fitted with a new tender incorporating a half-cab, as seen here on 9th September 1968.
(Festiniog Railway Archives)

8.   An April 1969 picture, which, in the opinion of the author captures the magic of the restored FR, shows the 1879 built Fairlie Patent double-engine locomotive *Earl of Merioneth* shunting carriage no. 17, a Brown Marshalls six compartment bogie coach of 1876, and known as a bowsider. Britannia Terrace is in the background and the scene is enhanced as all the track is laid with double head rails, which had been such a notable feature of the railway in pre-preservation days. (J.B.Snell)

9.   Turning 45 degrees right from the last picture and looking at the Britannia Foundry, double-engine *Earl of Merioneth* is seen shunting stock in April 1971. The locomotive was built in 1886 and named *Livingston Thompson*. It was renamed *Taliesin* in 1932 and finally *Earl of Merioneth* in 1961. This engine was withdrawn from service later in the year this photograph was taken and today is a non-working exhibit. (Michael Whitehouse)

← 10. *Merddin Emrys* is coming slowly around the sharp curve into the station on 2nd August 1969, with the prominent, but plain and functional offices which had replaced the historic Britannia Foundry, in the background. (Robin Patrick)

← 11. A busy scene at Portmadoc in 1971 shows two trains and the goods shed on the right with track still laid into it, and on the extreme right, the points for the former Welsh Highland line lead towards the Britannia Bridge. On the left is 2-6-2T *Mountaineer* built at the Cooke Works of the American Locomotive Company, New Jersey, USA, in 1917, for the War Department Light Railways. After the War it was sold to the Tramway de Pithiviers à Touray and when that railway closed in 1964, it was bought by John Ransom, who donated it to the FR in 1967. During 1971 the locomotive was converted to burn oil and its smoke box and chimney (with spark arrester fitted) painted aluminium. To the right is ex Penrhyn Quarry 0-4-0STT *Blanche* making ready to depart for Tan-y-Bwlch.
(Festiniog Railway Archives)

12. The two 'Penrhyn Ladies' are double heading a train which is waiting to depart from Portmadoc sometime in early 1971. The modifications made by the FR to these locomotives are readily apparent. Leading is *Linda* with her open backed cab, whilst *Blanche* behind, has a tender fitted with a cab, thus giving the footplate crew much better protection against the elements when running downhill.
(Festiniog Railway Archives)

PORTHMADOG

13.   Large crowds turned out in 1979 to celebrate the centenary of *Merddin Emrys*, the oldest working Fairlie double engine in service. Alongside is the FR designed double-engine built at Boston Lodge in 1979, *Earl of Merioneth*. (Festiniog Railway Archives)

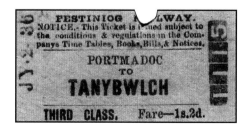

14.   This view also dating from 1979, shows the changing scene at what had become Porthmadog, in 1974. The 2-6-2T *Mountaineer* gets under way from the station. The locomotive has its original FR loading gauge cab, which it retained for another four years, and a bell on top of the smokebox. Behind on the left, there is now an extension between the original station and the goods shed, built in 1974, and on the right the Britannia Foundry has gone, demolished in 1972. (Peter Johnson coll.)

15.   Three of these carriages, nos 3, 4 and 5 are survivors of the first passenger vehicles on a narrow gauge railway in the world. They were built by Brown, Marshalls of Birmingham in 1863/64, having a closed single compartment with knifeboard seats for fourteen 3rd class passengers, whilst no. 6 is a semi open carriage. (Festiniog Railway Archives)

The Cob

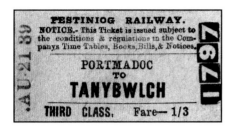

16.   A classic Festiniog scene! *Prince* is making his way across the Cob towards Boston Lodge with stock in both the green and ivory and varnished teak liveries on 20th September 1966. In the background the prominent hill of Meol-y-Gest rising to 860 feet (262m) above sea level, stands sentinel over Portmadoc. (Festiniog Railway Archives)

➔   17. Contrasting Fairlie Patent double engines are seen crossing the Cob en route from Boston Lodge to Portmadoc Harbour. Leading is the cab-less *Merddin Emrys* which had been returned to traffic in 1961 after an extensive, but unfinished overhaul. With its new welded side tanks painted in red oxide lead primer, it is leading the recently renamed *Earl of Merioneth*. This view is looking south east towards Boston Lodge and shows the impressive structure of William Maddocks embankment, completed in 1811. It is 1600 yards long and enabled land reclamation in the River Glaslyn estuary. (Festiniog Railway Archives)

BOSTON LODGE

18.   Looking north westwards from the hill behind Boston Lodge, *Linda* is at the end of the Cob, passing the entrance to Boston Lodge. Visible inside the yard is the other 'Penrhyn Lady', *Blanche*, and the long slate roofed building, used since preservation days as a locomotive running shed until demolished in 1988. The extensive marshes of the Glaslyn estuary and the land reclaimed from the sea, with Tremadoc visible on the far side, form an impressive landscape.
(Festiniog Railway Archives)

19.　　Coming around the curve at Pen Cob and passing the entrance to Boston Lodge on 6th April 1969, *Earl of Merioneth* now faces a 1 in 90 gradient towards Minffordd. (Robin Patrick)

→ 20. The first two weeks of preservation service was operated by the ex-War Department 1917 built Simplex. It is seen here at Boston Lodge Halt, at the end of the one mile journey from Harbour Station. The fare was 1/- return (5p) or 8d single (3.5p). Today, the small car, an Austin A30, is also of interest to motoring enthusiasts! (J.B. Snell)

→ 21. This is the first Fairlie double-engine built at Boston Lodge in 1879 and was the last to be used up to closure of the railway in 1946. However, during the closure period *Merddin Emrys* was left with water in its tanks and wet coal slack in its bunkers, which caused severe corrosion. A new set of welded side tanks were necessary before it could re-enter service. The locomotive is seen in August 1961, running with its new tanks in undercoat paint and without its cab. (Michael Whitehouse coll.)

22. In July 1962, *Linda*, one of three main line locomotives of the Penrhyn Quarry Railway which had closed the previous month, arrived by rail from Port Penrhyn to Minffordd. In August 1963, still in PQR livery of black, lined blue and red, she is seen in the yard attached to an old George England tender and fitted with vacuum brakes. (Gordon Monks)

23. *Linda* is inside the erecting shop under repair. Her boiler was superheated in 1969, a leading pony truck was fitted in 1970 and she was converted to oil firing in 1971. The frames of sister engine *Blanche* are seen in the foreground. (Michael Whitehouse coll.)

24.   The American built 2-6-2T *Mountaineer*, which had been converted to oil firing, was photographed on 7th August 1972 from a window in the offices at Boston Lodge and is passing the yard with an up train to Dduallt. (John Alexander)

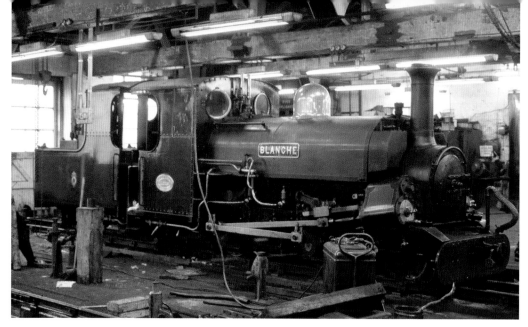

25.   *Blanche* is seen inside Boston Lodge in 1981 fitted with her tender cab, leading pony truck and FR type sand boxes in front of the saddle tank. Also prominent are the cylinders fitted in 1972 with outside admission piston valves in place of the original slide valves. (Peter Johnson)

26.   Two Fairlie double-engines, *Merddin Emrys* and *Earl of Merioneth* with a returning special train to Porthmadog are seen below Rhiw Plas Bridge and nearing Boston Lodge on 4th May 1980. (John Alexander)

MINFFORDD

27.   An interesting work-a-day scene, an activity not usually seen by many visitors to the railway, was an FR coal train at Minffordd. Here, *Moelwyn* is setting out down the main line to Boston Lodge with locomotive coal from Minffordd yard where British Railways had delivered it in August 1961. BR closed their yard and standard gauge sidings in 1972, so inevitably thereafter, coal deliveries to the FR had to be by road. (J.B. Snell)

28.   A truly rural scene as *Moelwyn* slowly eases down the curve into Minffordd Yard and exchange sidings in 1964. (Festiniog Railway Archives)

29.   This is a view of the British Railways single platform station at Minffordd in October 1964, with its attractive Cambrian Railways wooden buildings and the points leading to the FR exchange sidings. BR Standard Class 3 2-6-2T no. 82000 is shunting. (Festiniog Railway Archives)

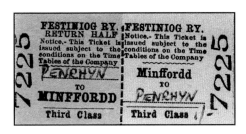

30.　At Minffordd in 1968 the thrice named double-engine *Earl of Merioneth* (originally *Livingston Thomson* then *Taliesin*) is shunting an engineers train back down the long siding leading to Minffordd yard. (Festiniog Railway Archives)

31.   This 2-4-0DM was built by Baldwin Locomotive Works, USA, in 1918 as a 45 hp 0-4-0 petrol locomotive for the French Government Artillery Railways. It was bought by the FR in 1925 and overhauled in 1956 and fitted with a diesel engine. It was rebuilt as a 2-4-0 and named *Moelwyn*. In November 1968 it is shunting at Minffordd going into the exchange sidings and taking *Linda's* boiler to the yard. From there the boiler was despatched by road to Hunslet Engine Co. at Leeds for the fitting of a new superheater and firebox.
(Festiniog Railway Archives)

→ 32. En route from static display at Butlins Holiday Camp Penychain, near Pwllhelli to Derby, the preserved LMS class 7P Pacific 6203 *Princess Margaret Rose* is being propelled slowly by no. 24053 (not visible) through Minffordd station on 11th May 1975, overseen from the FR station by *Merddin Emrys*. A young boy is gazing in awe at the size of an engine unlikely to be seen here again!
(Ken Robinson)

→ 33. A resplendent, as always, *Linda* is pulling out of Minffordd station on 31st August 1976 with the 10.15 train from Porthmadog to Dduallt. (Alan Wild)

34.   By the time of this picture on 31st July 1979, much of the FR main line had been relaid with flat bottomed rails, as seen here with *Linda* running into Minffordd station with a train for Tanygrisiau. The operating practice of the FR is for trains to run into the right-hand loop, the opposite of usual UK railway method. In the authors opinion, the double head rail in chairs attached to the sleepers as previously used by the FR, had enhanced the appearance and character of the railway. (Robin Patrick)

→ 35. A 1980 scene at the junction of the branch down into Minffordd yard and the exchange sidings, shows the main line to Porthmadog on the left. *Prince* is standing on the siding which forms a long head shunt, with a train being loaded with materials. (Festiniog Railway Archives)

→ 36. On 6th March 1982 the fireman is extracting the train staff from the token machine installed in Minffordd station. (Festiniog Railway Archives)

Gwyndy Bank

37.　　A view of the dry-stone embankment and arched bridge over the minor road at Gwyndy is seen from the south side, as *Linda*, in her 2-4-0ST guise, is hauling a train from Porthmadog to Dduallt on a beautiful Spring day in April 1974. (Michael Whitehouse)

38.　　Another view of the embankment and bridge at Gwyndy, but this is taken from the north side as a special train hauled by the two double-engines *Merddin Emrys* and *Earl of Merioneth* climb towards Penrhyn on 4th May 1980. (John Alexander)

PENRHYN

39. *Linda* is with a down train to Portmadoc. The station reopened in 1957 after a short loop had been constructed. It became the terminus of the railway for a year, until the next stage up to Tan-y-Bwlch was ready. The loop remained in situ for some years, but after a new signal box and loop at Rhiw Goch, a mile to the north, came into use in 1975, the Penrhyn loop and staff instruments were removed in 1981. (Festiniog Railway Archives)

40.   Another view at Penrhyn station in November 1974 has *Linda* working an up train. As volunteer numbers coming to the railway increased, more hostel accommodation was required. That at Harbour Station was limited, so in 1968 the Festiniog Railway Society started to renovate the station buildings here and convert them to a hostel, which was opened in 1972. (Festiniog Railway Archives)

41.   A picture contrasting the two Fairlie double-engines operating on the railway in the early 1980s. Left is *Merddin Emrys* which had been converted to oil burning in 1972 and the brand new *Earl of Merioneth* showing what was, to many, its extremely austere lines and a break from tradition. (Festiniog Railway Archives)

42.　　In an attractive setting *Merddin Emrys* slowly comes down the 1 in 82 gradient towards the level crossing over the A4085 road from Penrhyndeudraeth to Beddgelert, in October 1981. (Peter Johnson)

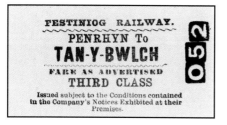

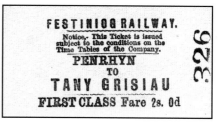

Rhiw Goch

43.　　Seen from Rhiw Goch, *Merddin Emrys* is coming down the side of the valley towards Penrhyn between mileposts 4 and 3.(Festiniog Railway Archives)

44.   We are looking towards Tan-y-Bwlch just beyond milepost 4, and before the new loop and signal box was brought into use in 1975. From the opening of the railway in 1836 this was one of four crossing loops provided for the exchange of horses between loaded downhill gravity slate trains and empty uphill wagons. Separate contractors and their horses worked each section, and the method was for the downhill horse to ride and rest in the horse dandy wagon at the rear of the train, and then return, hauling the empties back to their starting loop, where the operation was repeated. (Festiniog Railway Archives)

➜   45. After steam replaced horse traction, Rhiw Goch became redundant as its isolated position meant it had no use as a passenger station. By 1975, following the growth of passenger traffic, the service was outgrowing the existing station crossing loops. To improve line capacity, the loop was reinstated and a new signal box and siding constructed, so helping towards evening out the distance between block sections. In June 1975 the signalman holds up the staff for the fireman of the approaching *Merddin Emrys* to collect, shortly after the loop had been opened. (Festiniog Railway Archives)

➜   46. In November 1975, *Blanche* is entering Rhiw Goch loop with an uphill train, running left hand, and passing the colour light signals provided here for bi-directional running. (Festiniog Railway Archives)

← 47. A train hauled by *Linda* on 31st August 1968 is crossing Cei Mawr embankment bound for Dduallt. This very imposing stone embankment , 62 feet high from stream to rail level, is situated in an isolated position near Rhiw Goch. (John Alexander)

48.   Another historic view of *Merddin Emrys* shows coaching stock in the early preservation era livery crossing Cei Mawr, bound for Dduallt in about 1971. (Michael Whitehouse coll.)

49.   *Merddin Emrys* had re-turned to service in 1961 and is seen here with its train in the early preservation livery of green and cream with red ends, comprising mostly early bogie passenger coaches.
(Michael Whitehouse coll.)

➔   50. Cei Mawr is seen in August 1971 from the north-east side as *Mountaineer* comes across with a Portmadoc to Dduallt train. By the time of this picture *Mountaineer* had been fitted with a side window cab, but was still a coal burner, hence the ugly spark arrester attachment to the chimney. In addition, the smokebox door was painted with a heat resisting aluminium paint and crowned with a bell, the latter being merely added for cosmetic reasons. (Peter Johnson coll.)

51.　　Continuing uphill, *Linda* is seen just beyond Cei Mawr steadily climbing the 1 in 82 towards milepost 5 and on to Tan-y- Bwlch. (Festiniog Railway Archives)

52. In the attractive setting near cutting Budr, just past milepost 5, *Linda* continues up the constant 1 in 82 gradient towards Tan-y-Bwlch during Easter 1971. (Festiniog Railway Archives)

53. The afternoon train from Tan-y-Bwlch back to Portmadoc was hauled by *Taliesin*, on 16th May 1959. It comes around Sheepfold Curve, a lovely sight to inspire enthusiasm for this historic narrow gauge railway. The effort by the pioneers who helped in the resurrection of this outstanding railway is highly regarded. (Peter W. Gray)

PLAS HALT

54.   On an Autumn day in 1981, *Merddin Emrys* pauses at Plas Halt, which had been opened in June 1963 to serve the Plas Tan-y-Bwlch Estate. The mansion is now used as a residential study and educational centre. (Peter Johnson)

➔   55. *Prince* is coming around the fold in the hills above the artificial lake, Llyn Mair, at Whistling Curve in the course of turning 180 degrees on 18th May 1959. *Prince* is hauling a WHR bogie coach with three 'bug boxes', original four-wheel 1863/64 carriages, and an unidentified last vehicle to Tan-y-Bwlch. The driver seems to be having difficulty with greasy rails, and the fireman is standing on the buffer-beam hand sanding from the sand pots situated in front of the saddle tank. (Peter W. Gray)

➔   56. Ten years later, on 6th April 1969, *Blanche* is coming down hill at Whistling Curve hauling bogie stock in the era when carriages were painted in the varnished teak livery. Next to the engine is no. 100, the observation coach built in 1965, the first of a new series of corridor connected full loading gauge bogie carriages known as 'Century' stock to commemorate the 1865-1965 passenger train centenary. (Robin Patrick)

TAN-Y-BWLCH

57.   It was a major achievement that the railway was able to reopen to Tan-y-Bwlch on 5th April 1958, less than three years from the start in July 1955, and so making the route a distance of 7.5 miles. This shows *Prince* at Tan-y-Bwlch with its train of four -wheelers, often known as 'bug-boxes', in the first FR preservation livery of ivory and green. (Michael Whitehouse coll.)

➜   58. Prince is easing up to couple onto its train prior to the return journey to Portmadoc. The van is part of the 'Flying Flea', a summer relief train. (Michael Whitehouse coll.)

➜   59. A wonderful nostalgic scene of the early preservation days of the FR - what better than to see a Fairlie double-engine and two of its best known personalities in the sylvan unspoilt surroundings at Tan-y-Bwlch station? Former Kings Cross top-link driver Bill Hoole is having a chat in September 1958 with Bessie Jones, the station mistress, before Bill joins *Taliesin* to take his train back to Portmadoc. (Michael Whitehouse coll.)

60.   As previously mentioned, *Merddin Emrys* was the last double Fairlie in service when the railway closed in 1946. It required extensive rebuilding before it could re-enter traffic in 1961 and initially ran in red primer and without its cab, so presenting a most unusual sight. This interesting picture not only shows the firemans position on his side of the firebox, but also the angle of the two separate regulator handles. (Festiniog Railway Archives)

61.   Another vintage picture shows *Merddin Emrys* in his red undercoat cab-less days after return to service in 1961. (Festiniog Railway Archives)

62.   We are looking north from the south end of Tan-y-Bwlch station at the two 'Penrhyn Ladies', *Linda* and *Blanche*, attracting admirers prior to departure back to the coast. Note that all the track is laid with double head rails keyed in chairs and that the goods siding with its solitary slate wagon today forms part of the 'play area' adjacent to the café, formerly the goods shed. (Festiniog Railway Archives)

63.   The 1886 Boston Lodge built Fairlie double-engine *Earl of Merioneth* is taking water from the old tank at Tan-y-Bwlch. It was withdrawn from service in 1971 and its bogies and nameplates transferred to a new double-engine in 1979. Later cosmetically restored to its 1910 condition for display at the National Railway Museum in 1988, it returned to the FR in 2004 as an exhibit in time for the 50th anniversary of the revived FR. (Michael Whitehouse coll.)

64.   In bright Autumn light during November 1976, the 1918 Baldwin 2-4-0DM *Moelwyn* is engaged on permanent way work at Tan-y-Bwlch, preparing to haul a new point off a wagon to replace existing track. (Festiniog Railway Archives)

➔ 65.   Just before Tan-y-Bwlch station the railway crosses over the B4410 road to Beddgelert on a skew bridge with cast iron beams which bear the title 'Boston Lodge Foundry 1854'. In July 1979 the newly built oil-fired Fairlie double-engine, *Earl of Merioneth*, is on the bridge taking part in deflection tests. (Festiniog Railway Archives)

Above Tan-y-Bwlch

66.　　*Blanche* is coming over the stone embankment at Creuau on 6th April 1969, then onto the hillside above Tafarntrip on the far side of the valley. The train has just taken a mile to loop around to Tan-y-Bwlch station and to gain height on gradients of 1 in 80/90. (Robin Patrick)

67.　　Looking the other way to the previous picture, *Earl of Merioneth* is coming downhill from Dduallt and is approaching Tan-y-Bwlch in May 1968. Behind the engine is bogie coach no. 11, which in 1957/58 had been rebuilt as an observation saloon with end windows and, next to it, is no. 12 which was fitted with a buffet counter. (Gordon Monks)

68.	In 1969, with some rhododendrons adding a splash of colour to the scene, *Earl of Merioneth* is working hard on the ledge above the man-made lake Llyn Mair, and approaching Garnedd Tunnel. (Festiniog Railway Archives)

69.	*Earl of Merioneth* is emerging from the 60-yard long Garnedd Tunnel with a train from Dduallt to Portmadoc in May 1968. This illustrates the tight bore of the tunnel, which is the major factor that has determined the FR loading gauge. The space to the right indicates the route that the original railway took around the rocky outcrop prior to the tunnel being constructed in the early 1850s. (Gordon Monks)

70.   *Blanche* is seen approaching Garnedd Tunnel with a train from Dduallt to Portmadoc on 31st August 1968. In this area, spectacular views are obtained and looking east is the panorama of the Vale of Ffestiniog and mountains in part of the Snowdonia National Park. (John Alexander)

71.   *Blanche* again in August 1968, this time heading north beyond Garnedd Tunnel towards Dduallt, with magnificent views from the train looking south into the Vale of Ffestiniog and the River Dwyryd hundreds of feet below. (John Alexander)

72.   A picturesque scene as *Linda* is passing Coed-y-Bleiddiau, half way between Tan-y-Bwlch and Dduallt in June 1977. Between the two World Wars the property was let as a holiday home and one of its tenants was John Philby, the distinguished Arabist, who was the father of Kim Philby the notorious spy and traitor. (Festiniog Railway Archives)

73.   A classic Festiniog Railway train and setting is seen as *Earl of Merioneth* comes around Dduallt Curve on 31st August 1968 passing an old water tank at milepost 9 on the approach to Campbell's Platform. Behind the train is Moelwyn Mawr, rising to 2526 feet asl. (John Alexander)

74. *Blanche* is nearing Dduallt with the 13.15 train from Porthmadog just after a light snowfall on 27th March 1975. (Alan Wild)

75.   On the approach to Dduallt the railway is over 500 feet above sea level, thus enabling good views from the train. *Linda* is approaching Dduallt with the 14.15 train from Porthmadog on 19th August 1976. (Alan Wild)

DDUALLT

76.   On the final 1 in 86 climb to terminate at Dduallt on 29th August 1976, *Merddin Emrys* is passing the upper quadrant home signal with the 15.15 train from Porthmadog. (Alan Wild)

← 77. Looking the other way from the last picture on the same date, *Merddin Emrys* has just passed under the Rhoslyn Bridge which carries the new spiral of the deviation over the existing line at Dduallt. It is working the 14.17 train back to Porthmadog. (Alan Wild)

← 78. This undated scene at Dduallt, looking north, shows that early reconstruction of the line in the station area is to hand. (Festiniog Railway Archives)

79.   Just over a year after the railway was re-opened to Dduallt, there was a good crowd of passengers on the platform who have taken advantage of the steadily increasing route mileage and to inspect the progress of the deviation works. The columns and crossbeams of Rhoslyn Bridge were erected some five months before this picture was taken on 12th June 1969. It forms part of the only railway spiral in this country. (Festiniog Railway Archives)

80.　　On an extremely wet day in January 1976 0-4-0DM *Moel Hebog* has arrived from Tan-y-Bwlch with a tunnel clearance train, which had been checking alignments in Garnedd Tunnel. This little 70 h.p. locomotive was built by Hunslet in 1955 for the National Coal Board and was purchased by the FR in 1969. It is named after a mountain 2566 feet high and just to the south west of Beddgelert. (John Alexander)

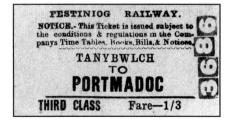

Above Dduallt

81.   This is the south end of the old and very wet Moelwyn Tunnel seen in October 1963. It was 730 yards long and opened on 24th May 1842. It was cut through very hard rock and took 2½ years to complete by means of hand tools, candles, black powder and use of horses. (Festiniog Railway Archives)

82.   This is looking out of the south end of the old Moelwyn Tunnel and gives a good impression of the wet, narrow bore and unlined sides of the tunnel. (Festiniog Railway Archives)

83.   The incredible achievements of the volunteer deviationists building the new line, requiring both a spiral and tunnel, has been well documented and this helps illustrate the enormity of the works. This shows Rhoslyn Bridge with its columns and decking finished but the embankments to each side still under construction during 1969. (Festiniog Railway Archives)

III.   This 1973 map indicates the alignment and lengths of the new and old tunnels, together with the position of the incline that preceded them. The new terminus at Blaenau Ffestiniog was eventually built on the former GWR station site and not as shown. The CEA had become the Central Electricity Generating Board. (M.Seymour)

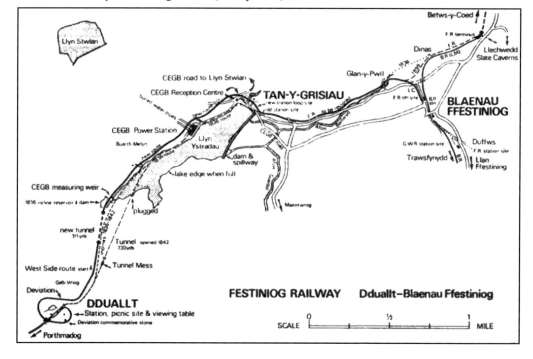

84. The deviation is seen under construction near milepost 10, looking north.
(Festiniog Railway Archives)

85.   The deviation is steadily progressing north at Gelliwog in May 1973, whilst on the right, the stone walls emphasise just how narrow the old Festiniog formation was.
(Festiniog Railway Archives)

86.   This is the scene of the work in hand at the deep cutting leading towards the south end of the new tunnel in October 1973. The deviation has raised the new line 35 feet above the old railway. (Peter Johnson)

87.   Work was also in progress on the north side of the new tunnel and it was just as labourious, as is seen with this skip being manhandled near the remains of Archer Dam during April 1974. (Michael Whitehouse)

88.   Skips are lined up in the cutting in June 1975 waiting for the excavator to scoop up rock for removal from near the tunnel mouth. (Festiniog Railway Archives)

89.   This is looking the other way from the previous picture with loaded skips being drawn away from the site. The open space on the right was later used for screening the rock excavated from the cutting. (Festiniog Railway Archives)

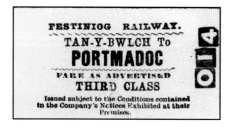

FESTINIOG RAILWAY.

TAN-Y-BWLCH To
PORTMADOC

FARE AS ADVERTISED
THIRD CLASS

Issued subject to the Conditions contained
in the Company's Notices Exhibited at their
Premises.

FESTINIOG RAILWAY

TAN-Y-BWLCH to
PORTMADOC

FARE AS ADVERTISED
THIRD CLASS SINGLE

Issued subject to the Conditions contained
in the Company's Notices Exhibited at their
Premises.

90.   By the time of this picture in 1976, the new preliminary tunnel was bored through 287 yards of rock, but there was still much work to be done before the tunnel was ready for trains. The sign board was a joke; the initials were those of Paul Dukes and Ron Leicester, who were members of staff who were involved in the construction. (Peter Johnson)

91.   'The Deviationists' seen here were some of the volunteers of both sexes and all walks of life, who gave up their time to come to this remote place, often in hostile weather, to work on the construction and help the railway achieve its ambition of returning to Blaenau Ffestiniog. (Festiniog Railway Archives)

92.   Part of the snow-capped Moelwyn Mountains are seen to best advantage on a crisp winter's day in January 1977. The 1842-1956 alignment of the railway towards Tanygrisiau is visible as a causeway when the reservoir, Llyn Ystradau, water level is low. The new railway route can be seen traversing left to right across the picture heading towards the Tanygrisiau Power Station. (Peter Johnson coll.)

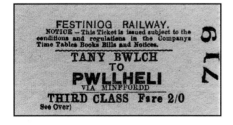

FESTINIOG RAILWAY.
NOTICE — This Ticket is issued subject to the
conditions and regulations in the Companys
Time Tables Books Bills and Notices.

TANY BWLCH
TO
PWLLHELI
VIA MINFFORDD

THIRD CLASS Fare 2/0
See Over)

719

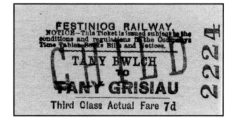

FESTINIOG RAILWAY.
NOTICE—This Ticket is issued subject to the
conditions and regulations in the Companys
Time Tables Books Bills and Notices.

TANY BWLCH
To
TANY GRISIAU

Third Class Actual Fare 7d

2224

93.   In May 1977, work was progressing to finish the south portal and 'shotcrete' (spray with concrete) the interior of the tunnel and attend to drainage, prior to the first gauging train into the tunnel on 28th May 1977. (Peter Johnson)

94.   In May 1977 2-4-0 DM *Moelwyn* brings a long train of spoil wagons around the spiral and over Rhoslyn Bridge shortly before the next section of the railway as far as Llyn Ystradau was open for passengers. (Peter Johnson)

95.　　On 25th June 1977, there is a large crowd gathered to witness Mr. Dafydd Elis-Thomas, the MP for Merionnydd, celebrate cutting of the tape to allow the first train through the new Moelwyn Tunnel. It was hauled by *Merddin Emrys*. (Festiniog Railway Archives)

96.   This country's only spiral at Dduallt is an excellent location to watch the trains coming uphill to gain the 35 feet necessary to reach the elevation of the new tunnel. In September 1979 *Mountaineer* is working hard as it comes up the 1 in 80 gradient over the Rhoslyn Bridge with a train to Tanygrisiau. Below, on the left, is Dduallt station which the train has just left.
(Peter Johnson coll.)

97.   The start of the deviation and new line commences at the north end of Dduallt station and sweeps round to make the spiral at the south end of the station. Here double heading by *Merddin Emrys* and the 1979 built *Earl of Merioneth* are starting to climb towards the spiral in this undated view, which is believed to be a special train to Tanygrisiau in May 1980. (Festiniog Railway Archives)

98.   Standing on Dduallt station platform we can see *Merddin Emrys* working the 11.35 train from Porthmadog to Tanygrisiau. It has turned nearly 360 degrees by means of the spiral and is heading towards Moelwyn Tunnel on 30th August 1981. (Author)

↓ 99. *Linda* is working hard as she comes out of Moelwyn Tunnel with the 13.20 train from Porthmadog on 30th August 1981. (Author)

100. A view looking across the valley has *Mountaineer* heading back to Porthmadog and the old Wrysgan Quarry incline prominent on the mountainside behind the train. The incline to this quarry dates from the 1850s and had the unusual feature of going into a tunnel at the top, with the quarry out of sight on the other side. The quarry and incline were worked up until 1946. At this point the train is on a rising 1 in 78 gradient for a short distance towards the summit cutting, 669 feet above sea level. (John Alexander)

101.   Work is in progress in preparing the track bed over the level crossing at Stwlan Dam Road close by milepost 12. (Festiniog Railway Archives)

TANYGRISIAU

102.   This view was taken in May 1978 from Stwlan Dam Road looking down at the new Tanygrisiau platform and shows how the railway makes a reverse curve through the station. This was the terminus of the railway between June 1978 and May 1982. (Festiniog Railway Archives).

103.   The railway is seen as it was in May 1978, just before the re-opening to Tanygrisiau. There was a lot of work to be undertaken before trains can run on the ledge between the houses in the village. (Festiniog Railway Archives)

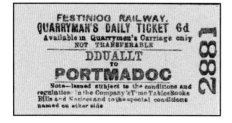

104.   Steadily getting there - just under another one and half miles to go! *Merddin Emrys* brings the re-opening train into Tanygrisiau on a very wet day on 24th June 1978. (Festiniog Railway Archives)

105.   Approaching Tanygrisiau station on 23rd September 1979, *Blanche* is coming around the curve and over the bridge spanning the River Cwmorthin and its adjacent waterfall with a train from Porthmadog. (John Alexander)

106.   A broadside view of the River Cwmorthin bridge and falls shows *Prince* departing with a train back to Porthmadog. The bridge was made with three Dow-Mac 55 feet long concrete beams and a 100-ton crane was hired to place them in position. (Festiniog Railway Archives)

107.   The railway at Tanygrisiau station is at a higher level than the old track, but as can be seen on 2nd August 1979, although it has a spacious platform it is bereft of facilities. *Mountaineer* makes ready to leave for Porthmadog. (Robin Patrick)

108.   *Blanche* is about to leave Tanygrisiau on its return journey back to Porthmadog one day in May 1981. (Peter Johnson)

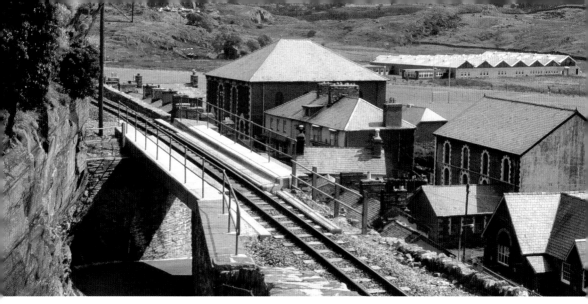

109.   The reinstated railway crosses a very steep and narrow road serving the upper part of Tanygrisiau on Dolrhedyn Bridge. In 1957 the County Council removed the bridge thinking that the railway would never return to Blaenau, so it had to be replaced with that seen here on a higher level in 1980, financed by grants. (Festiniog Railway Archives)

Below Blaenau Ffestiniog

110.   The approach to Blaenau Ffestiniog is over-shadowed by enormous slate waste tips as seen here, near milepost 13, where the railway crosses the River Barlwyd. To the left, the course of the original line of 1836 to Dinas was clearly discernible in October 1975.
(Festiniog Railway Archives)

111. Glan-y-Pwll civil engineering and permanent way depot is situated near milepost 13, half a mile west of Blaenau Ffestiniog station, and is seen in 1975. (Festiniog Railway Archives)

112. This is looking eastwards in the 1960s towards the former Great Western Railway Central station in Blaenau Ffestiniog showing the FR line towards the joint station and Duffws on the left, and the GWR goods shed on the right. Prominent is the diamond crossing of the narrow gauge track over the standard gauge rails. The FR line was to gain access to exchange sidings out of picture to the right of the goods shed whist the standard gauge track was purely a head shunt for the GWR goods yard. (Festiniog Railway Archives)

BLAENAU FFESTINIOG

113.   This is a comparison with the previous picture in about 1981. The Western Region branch from Bala Junction had closed to passengers in 1960 and to goods traffic a year later, so all trace of Central station has gone. However, the line to Trawsfynydd was re-opened in 1964 to convey nuclear flask traffic and this involved providing a connection between the two BR termini over the FR track seen on the left in picture no.112.   In its place the track bed for the FR station is being prepared on the right, and the footbridge over the new standard gauge station on the left is complete. (Festiniog Railway Archives)

114.   We are adjacent to the site of the former Great Western Central station and are looking from the new footbridge, seen in the previous picture, in October 1981. The land on the left is cleared for the FR track to be laid, whilst on the right the standard gauge run round loop and re-aligned track for the new British Railways station is in position. (Peter Johnson)

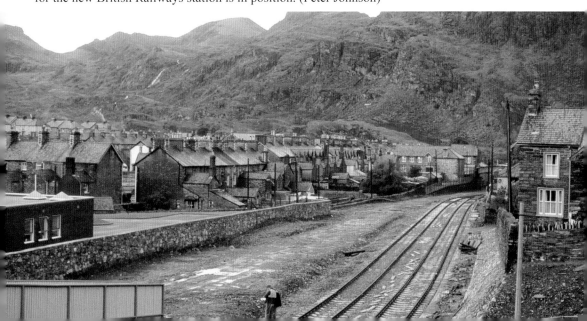

← 115. The new BR station was opened on 22nd March 1982, but the FR station was not yet ready for use. However, the FR had a works train hauled by *Blanche* coming to Blaenau Ffestiniog and it is seen approaching alongside the first scheduled BR passenger train into the brand new station. (Peter Johnson)

← 116. *Blanche* is now safely standing at the nearly completed FR station, whilst a small crowd has gathered and they are awaiting the train to move into position alongside the BR train for the celebratory photographs.
(Festiniog Railway Archives)

117. The promotional BR Diesel Multiple Unit, complete with a headboard to advertise the railway link between Llandudno Junction and Porthmadog stands alongside *Blanche* on 22nd March 1982. (Peter Johnson)

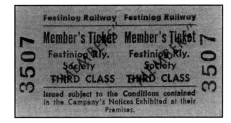

← 118. There was further interest that day when a class 40 approached the new BR station with a train of nuclear flasks from Trawsfynydd Power Station. This was situated on the remnant of the GWR branch to Bala, and the train is on its way down the Conwy Valley to the main line at Llandudno Junction. Construction of the nuclear power station commenced in 1959 and it was opened in 1968. Its reactors were shut down in 1991 and it is now decommissioned. (Festiniog Railway Archives)

← 119. Two months after the BR station was opened, the great day arrived for the Festiniog Railway and, after 27 years of hope, adversity and massive endeavour, at last the railway returned to Blaenau Ffestiniog on 25th May 1982. Despite a very wet day, large crowds were gathered on the new platform. John Routly, Chairman of the FR Company and FR Trust was able to welcome *Earl of Merioneth*, complete with headboard, into the station. Coincidentally, the re-opening took place 150 years and two days after the Act incorporating the Festiniog Railway Company was passed. (Festiniog Railway Archives)

120. Children have climbed onto the wall of the adjacent school to watch *Earl of Merioneth* move up into the headshunt to draw-up alongside a two car diesel multiple unit standing on the runround loop. Blaenau at last! (Festiniog Railway Archives)

MP Middleton Press

EVOLVING THE ULTIMATE RAIL ENCYCLOPEDIA

Easebourne Lane, Midhurst, West Sussex.
GU29 9AZ   Tel:01730 813169

www.middletonpress.co.uk   email:info@middletonpress.co.uk
A-978 0 906520 B- 978 1 873793 C- 978 1 901706 D-978 1 904474
E - 978 1 906008   F - 978 1 908174

All titles listed below were in print at time of publication - please check current availability by looking at our website - *www.middletonpress.co.uk* or by requesting a Brochure which includes our *LATEST* RAILWAY TITLES also our TRAMWAY, TROLLEYBUS, MILITARY and WATERWAYS series